BLACK SANDS
LEGENDS OF KEMET
The Coloring Book for Adults

By Manuel Godoy

Artist: David Lenormand

Editor: Geiszel Godoy

MISSION STATEMENT

To provide our brothers and sisters with images that represent them and their cultures.

Content

Section 1

Characters are in their stand up portraits

Section 2

Dynamic Poses for some characters and scenes

SPECIAL NOTICE

THE FIRST SECTION IS PORTRAIT ORIENTATION AND THE SECOND IS LANDSCAPE. YOU MUST TURN THE BOOK SIDEWAYS IN THE SECOND SECTION. PLEASE SKIP AROUND THE BOOK AND ENJOY YOURSELF.

Quarterly Competition

Good day extended family. As you may have heard, there is a competition held quarterly where fans get to upload their work on our deviant page for online competitions. We will select the top 10 of the quarter and have the community vote to decide who wins.

Winners will receive amazing rewards. An example would be a council membership slot which is a very unique item. You will have an in game sprite made in your image, as well as that character carrying a version of your name that is lore friendly. You will be able to tell all your friends; you are in Black Sands.

ACKNOWLEDGEMENTS

I would like to give a special shout out to the Ankh Life and the backers of my original gofundme that helped launch our effort to bringing the best black gaming experience imaginable. Without you, The Sands would have struggled for months to get this ball rolling and I will always remember you guys.

To the young boy and girls looking at this for the first time. I believe in you. This is about you. We need our own heroes, our own stories, and our own experiences. I look forward to seeing all your work.

USEFUL LINKS

BlackSandsCollection.com (Shop)

BlackSandsEntertainment.com (Gaming Official Website)

Facebook.com/blacksandsentertainment

Twitter.com/theblacksands

Rah, the Dark Pharaoh

Pantheon: Kemetic

Rah was the first mortal created by Nun. He was considered an experiment and was born with flaws. The objective of making mortals was to incorporate the power of the ancient bloodlines with a limited body. As a result, Rah had an unusually high amount of power and innate abilities uncommon to his kin. But the side effect is he suffers from hallucinations and spends most his time keeping the voices in his head in check. His fighting style is Martial Arts. He can also read any language for unknown reasons.

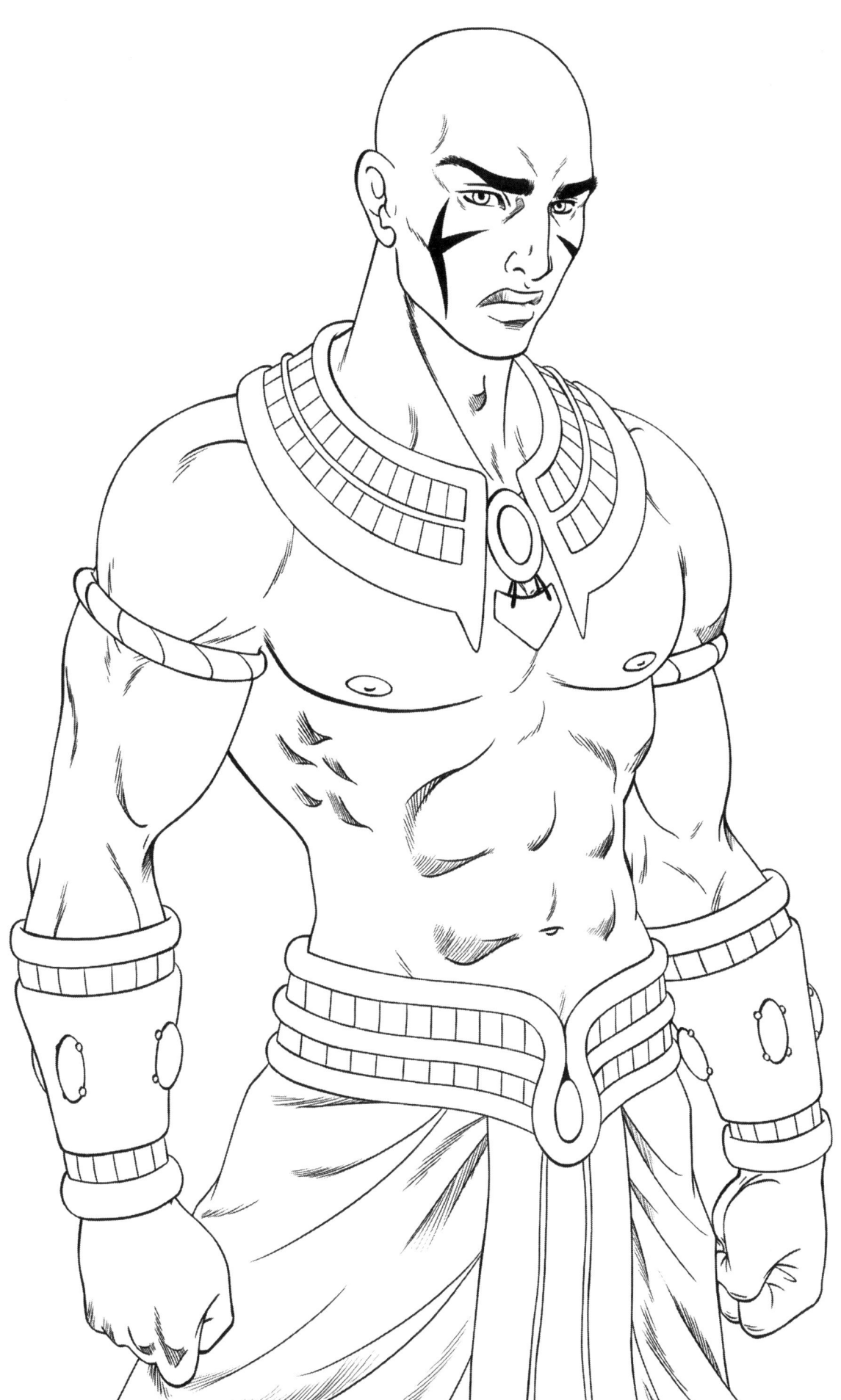

Amesemi, the Soul Chanter

Pantheon: Kushite

It cannot be said enough that magic is the rarest innate gift in the ancient bloodlines. Amesemi was blessed with the ability to control Fire and Wind. Nun noticed from a young age that she could do so and took her directly under him as his apprentice. There she learned about the ancient dialects and rituals of the pure bloodlines. She has not yet unlocked her potential though, as she fears the power she possesses cannot be controlled. Of all of Rah's kin, she is the one who is fixated on Rah's mental health the most. She fights with the elements

Apedemak, Pride of the Pack

Pantheon: Kushite

Created not too long after Rah, Apedemak is his brother and their rivalry is fierce. Since they were children, Apedemak was more of an emotional and just leader while Rah was cold and ruthless. Every time they would fight, Rah would obliterate him. Knowing that he did not have the strength to beat Rah, he has been developing his tactical skills to perhaps outwit Rah one day. As he got older, he became obsessed with Amesemi but he was unusually shy about it. Gilgamesh loves to taunt him into making a move. Apedemak, over time became second in command. Though he cannot beat Rah in a duel, he has perfected the art of skirmishing and now no fight is simple between the bitter rivals. He fights with Javelins and Spears.

Gilgamesh, the Whisperer

Pantheon: Sumerian

Gilgamesh was born, but I dare say he was not raised. The true meaning of a lone wolf, Gilgamesh seeks to follow no one. If there is something new, he must discover it. If there is danger, he must conquer it. The man is driven with a psychotic thrill for adventure. Being "trapped" in the rift has caused Gilgamesh to be irritable at times. He wants to explore and take on the challenges the world has to offer. You would think someone like this would love battle, but that is not him. He prefers to talk his way out of things. He is a true politician. Gilgamesh is one not to be trusted but his sense of adventure and wits can prove valuable to anyone brave enough to tag along. He fights with a whip and prefers to be mounted.

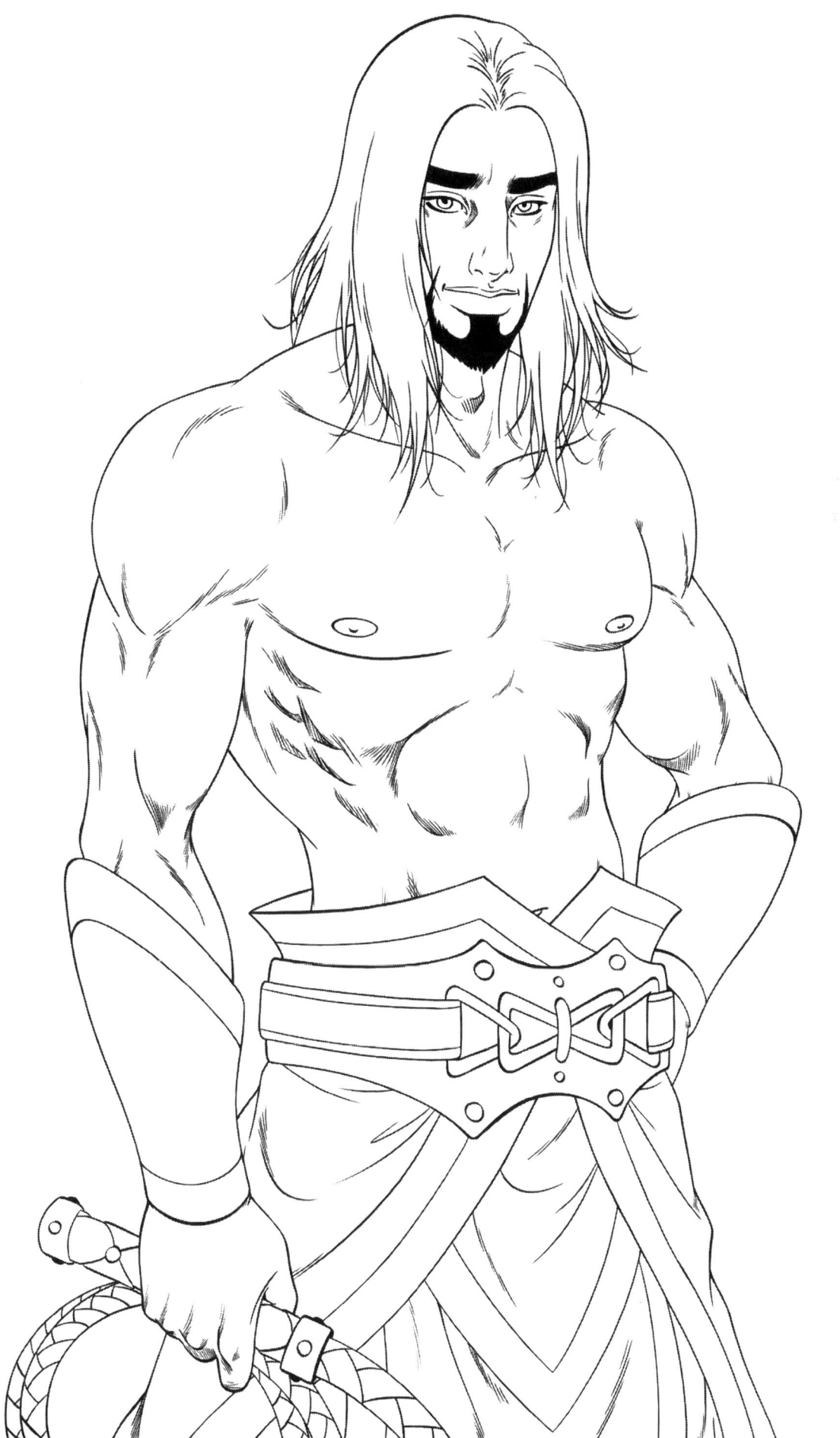

Bydos, the Boy Prodigy

Pantheon: Ethiopian

Bydos is a strange young man. He was created much later than the rest and cannot defeat any of his elders in battle but his ability to learn the techniques and tactics of the others is unparalleled. He can be considered a weapons master. Even with his exceptional skill and unlimited potential to grow, he has absolutely no leadership skills at all. He is the epitome of a soldier. Nun has studied the boy carefully and decided that Bydos would one day serve under one of the three when they are released from the rift. Unlike most, Bydos looks forward to his service to the others. He fights with all weapons available to him.

Nun, the Watcher

Pantheon: Kemetic

Nun is as alien being that was sent on a mission to advance both his people and those of earth. Known as the Watcher, Nun is the creator of all the ancient gods and the demi-gods currently in the rift. He is said to have been of a noble bloodline and rarely shows remorse in his actions. To him, the world is an experiment and when the experiment gets out of control, he corrects it. Nun is very powerful but is trapped in the Rift due to his genetic makeup being incompatible with the outside world. He longs for the day when he can take his final rest knowing his work was successful.

Coeus, The Fallen Prince

Pantheon: Greek

Thousands of years ago, the son of Uranus was marked with an ancient spirit known as the devourer. Uranus sought the council of Nun and Nun decided Coeus should be destroyed. Uranus, pitying his son, decided to instead imprison him. Marduk did not like his decision but agreed when Uranus allowed the Anunnaki to build the facility to guarantee he would never escape. Nun never knew he was kept alive, locked underground and chained for 1500 years. But now that the rift is unstable, the quakes have broken the chains on the prince. He is still imprisoned but how long could the facility last without the beast restrained?

Japetus, the Piercer

Pantheon: Greek

He was the last child of Gaia before her death. She knew not her son because he was still in his incubation pod when she set off to seek Nun. Kronus had suspicions when Gaia went missing and decided to not release Japetus until he knew the ware bouts of mother. The Incubation pod was a barrier protecting the host from contamination. Kronus knew that if he ever needed to get back into the Rift, only one that has never been soiled would be allowed to enter. When Rhea's secret was revealed to Kronus, he told Japetus, who was still trapped in his pod. Kronus then sent him on his way to the rift to find out what happened to his mother and claim his freedom.

Bakasura, The Flesh Walker

Pantheon: Hindu

Legend has it then once every 3000 years, a child of Nibiru is born with flesh. These children become super predators with hyper-concentrated muscle tissue and understone instead of bone. Their flesh allows them unparalleled speed and unlike the others before him, Bakasura has survived. Unlike on his world, where the planet was incinerated every 200 years, Earth is much calmer. His reign as a wild Asura has been long and all the ancient fear him for he devours both the ancient and the living. It is unclear if he has any instincts other than the hunt but one thing is for sure, avoid at all cost.

Vritra, Dragon King of the Asura

Pantheon: Hindu

Vritra was the rules of the Asura though the Asura had no unity among their people. The Deva used the actions of a few of the wilder Asura to condemn the rest and consorted with the Anunnaki and Titans to destroy them. In an effort to save his people, Vritra surrendered to the Deva. He knew his people stood no chance because they were not united under one cause. The Deva created a massive dimensional tare underground to house the most dangerous prison that ever existed and sealed all the Asura there for the rest of eternity. The Asura now knew the reality of their weakness from being such independent souls and if they were ever to get their chance again, they would unite under Vritra and put the Deva down for good.

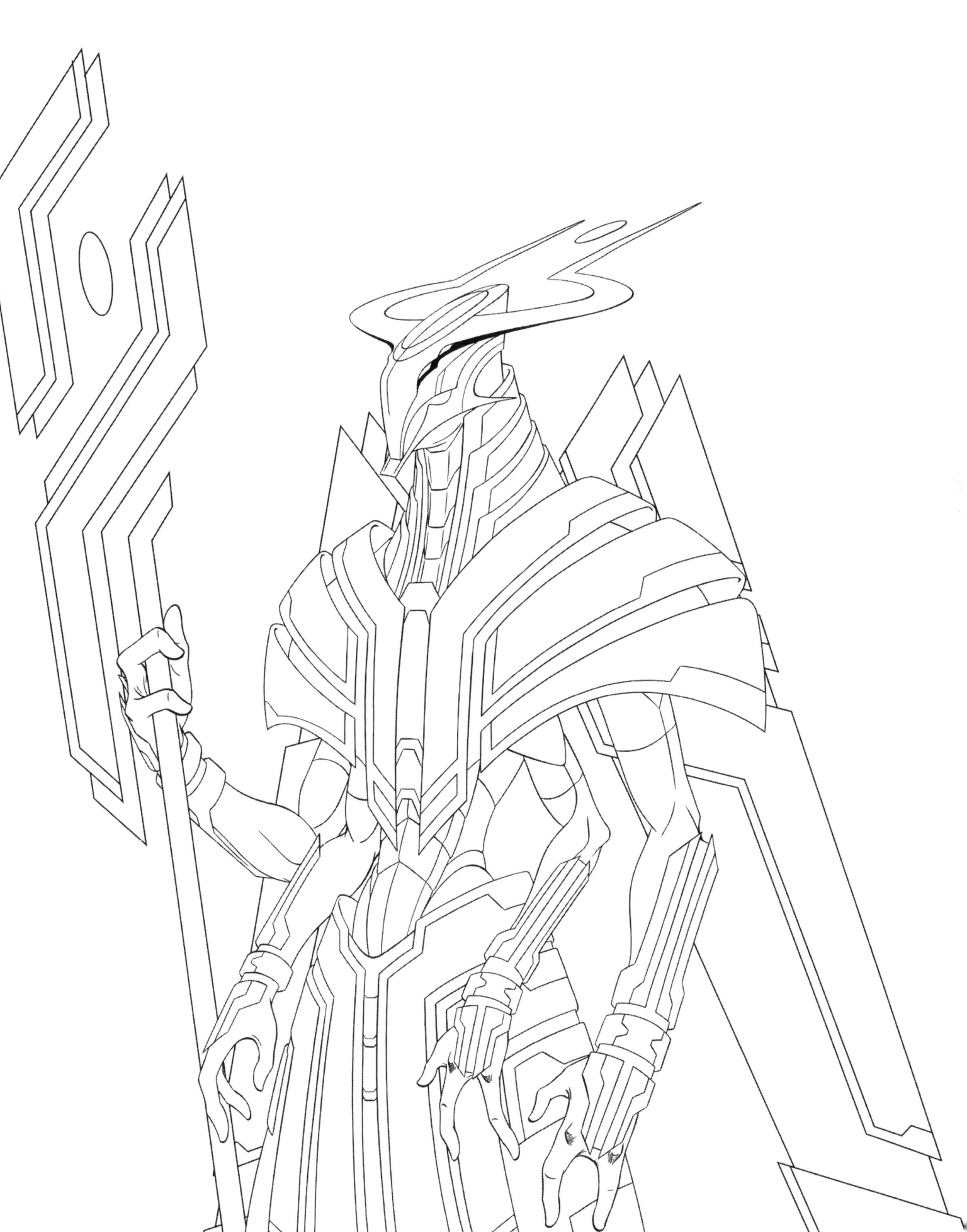

SECTION 2
Turn the Book into landscape orientation

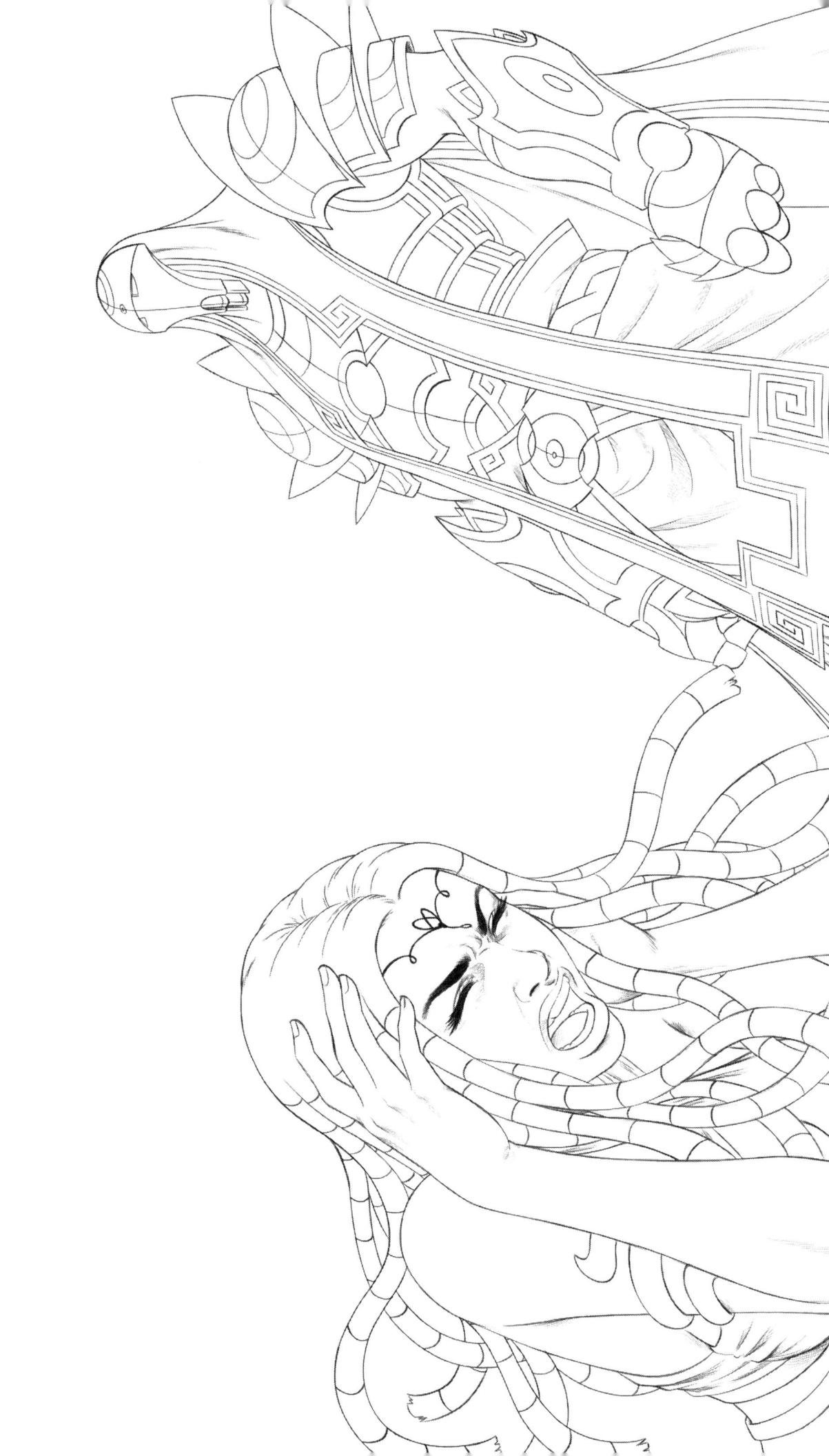

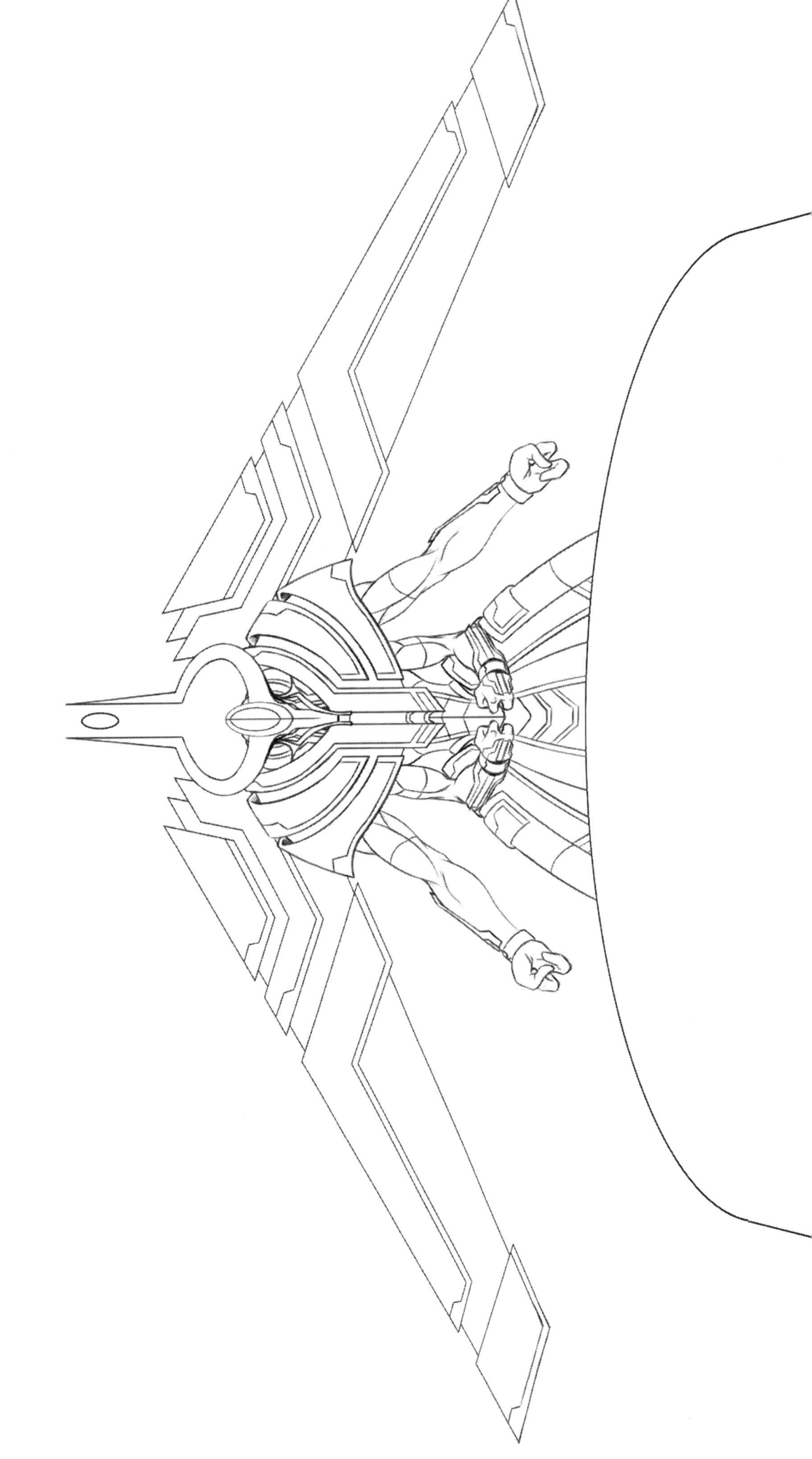

WE HOPE YOU ENJOYED YOUR BLACK SANDS EXPERIENCE

Be sure to upload your work on our deviant page.

We are all looking forward to it!